the color that made indigo

aubrey maru

ISBN: 979-8-9931205-1-5

Published by Aubrey Maru

Printed in the United States of America

before you begin

this collection speaks openly about abuse, betrayal, and survival. it is graphic, and it may feel too familiar. take care as you flip through and thanks for dropping by.

also - there is no happy ending here, it's just not how my story played out. maybe it hasn't happened yet, maybe it's just not meant to be. if my words sound anything like your life, i truly am pained for what you've gone through and hope you get your happy ending. if not, you're welcome to sit with me and hang out in the flames.

// aubrey

to the color that made indigo
you said my words are like knives
so i started writing them down for you
maybe one day it'll all get through

xo

fire

i want so badly to avenge the death of who you once were
to shatter your legs
and bludgeon you with your precious phone
set fire to your filthy ego
sever each fingertip so you may

n e v e r

feel flesh again
then string each finger to a necklace
as a forever reminder of your sins
the stench of rot your new signature cologne
that warns others of your deeds

no form of torture would come close
to the devastation you've inflicted
but i'll make do

//

i lied for you
they asked me to speak
to help them survive
and i lied for you

i made you smaller
so they wouldn't be afraid
so i wouldn't be pitied
so i wouldn't be the girl who stayed

i knew better
and every lie
tasted like blood
but your image
was more sacred
than my pain

now my fire has awoken
and craves to devour
your worthless flesh
i'm done bleeding quietly

i will no longer be silenced

//

you were a game of inverted roulette
five in the barrel and one chance you wouldn't kill me
you blew me apart over and over and over
and i kept running back to play again

//

love
isn't being terrified

love
isn't watching you throw a dinner plate
four inches from my skull
and me bending over to clean up the shards

love
isn't flooding the bathtub with tears
at four o'clock in the morning
because you're sleeping peacefully
and i still can't get your words out of my head

love
isn't watching you pack your bags
time and time again
and stack everything to the brim of your run-down car
just to unpack it all twenty minutes later

love
isn't losing all my hobbies and interests
because every time i pluck a string or hold a pen
i am told i am not good enough
that i will never be good enough

love
isn't lying to my friends
love
isn't what i'm in

so why can't i leave

//

you are poison laced with nicotine
a rose with powdered thorns
crown me your next victim
i'll build your throne to the clouds

//

you know you loved me
maybe it scared you
falling too fast
too hard
and you lost control

//

in teeth and tongue
you always knew where venom plays best
and i think i always knew
how dangerous you were

maybe i didn't mind
the gamble of loving a weapon
maybe the pain proved i was still alive

maybe i didn't mind
being your favorite wound
your willing mark
your place to sink your fangs
and drink me dry

in the bite
was a kind of worship
a godly connection
and the poison
was just more of you beneath my skin

so please
my breath is a gift
you can decide when to take

//

you were stardust in my lungs
a constellation i could trace
with my eyes closed
our souls became galaxies
some mythical story
people tell around campfires
as the smoke reaches for the stars

we were infinite

//

is this love or is this mania

//

being with you
contrary to my very core beliefs
is not living
this is no life
this is survival

it's an illness
i crave to be hunted
addicted to the adrenaline
shaking and begging
that you'll bleed me drier than you did the last time
that you'll snap my bones
into more shards than you have before
with watercolor bruises that stay with me to remind me of you
like the kisses you leave on my neck
cold, serrated words cutting into one ear
and dripping out the other
your fingertips wrapping around my airway
and slowly collapsing inward
with your grip releasing moments later
as you throw my skull through the drywall

after days of silence you whisper you love me
and i believe it

//

stop setting me on fire just to keep yourself warm

//

and i came back
and i came back
and i came back
a slave for your sorry ego
you didn't do a damn thing for me
and i gave my all to you

//

you never loved me
you loved the way i made you feel clean
that i could bleach away your sins
and conceal your consequences
that i'd scrub every drop of blood from the carpet
while you pull my hair and kiss me with your poison tongue

// *property*

you said my edge was a little sharp
so i filed it down for you
ignoring the drips of blood puddling on the floor
as i grated the edges of my soul to please you

you said i'm far too cold to touch
and though my chill is what allured you
i set fire to my heart of coal
and melted myself away

you said my darkness isn't gentle
that my mind could be more dainty
so i slit my throat, completely gutted myself
and surrendered my voice to you

i've sliced myself in pieces
let you choose the dotted lines
stitch by stitch
i deconstructed myself
into exactly the version you desired
a woman i never wanted to be
i loved the me that i was before you
i miss her
now i'm just a compilation of botch jobs
for the ever almighty ephemeral maniac

you are correct
in that you never did ask me to abuse myself so horrifically
though you held your own arena of abuse
i do own the ghastly acts i performed on myself
for you

but what kind of monster
looks his lover in the eye
hands her a carving knife
and smiles,
"*again*"

// *dude i was cool before i met you*

i gave you my trust
and you cracked it like glass
just to hear the sound

// for the plot

disgusting excuse for a man
tell me how you got so comfortable
lurking through the dark
preying on slimy flesh
and sinking back into the shadows

//

you cannot comprehend life beyond your own
only what's self gratifying to your carnal nature
something other men have learned to tame
while

you

chose to feed it
to dwell in it
to become it

you are filth
you are unholy
you are disgust

i cannot bear the burden of knowing you

//

you gravely disturbed soul
feasting on the blood of naivety
wearing the skin of your sacrifices
alluring monster
you will never be satiated

//

"it was only once"
as if that excuses the most putrescent sin
as if that was even true
as if your skin cells aren't still collecting under her acrylics
don't waste your breath
don't waste my time
we both know what you did

//

you refuse to unveil the truth
so i became a truth seeker
to a fault

my newly neurotic nature fixated on proving what you won't
i'm an embarrassment to myself
my waking hours spent chasing red string pinned to notecards
my sleep replaced by night terrors with nowhere left to escape

please put me out
i cannot stop my mind

// corkboard shrine to my unraveling

you call me a venomous villainess
because you showed up with dull hands
and no intention to love anything other than yourself

you can blame me until your tongue splits
like you didn't poison us from the inside out
just to prove you could

this didn't have to end in bloodshed
you had a woman who would have followed you anywhere
if you ever had anywhere to go

//

you told everyone you're homeless
so why do you still tug the bedding too far to your side
still whisper goodnight
still wish me luck as you head off to work in the morning

you told everyone we haven't been together for years now
so why's your skin still on my skin
your words still on my ears
your heart still on my soul

you told everyone you're the "potential" father
as if i was the one who committed the ultimate betrayal
as if you're not projecting
as if he's not a clone of you

you told everyone i'm crazy
psychotic
neurotic
as if i'm not running on adrenaline 24/7
as i dodge your endless words and fists

you told all your friends
and mine
what you want them to think
why are you so scared of telling the truth

//

you were never mine
you whored yourself out to the public
sweating anyone who would look your way
you sold your body for twenty six likes

was it everything you wanted

//

the crown you dropped between her legs
was never made of gold
just rusted tin
spit-shined by desperation
yet you still wore it like royalty

you are nothing
but cowardice with bad taste
a little boy in his father's shoes
stomping kingdoms into dust
as they question your delusional grandeur

no throne could ever be enough
for a boy still worshipping his own reflection

//

i should've buried you in the dirt
where your lies belong
let the worms learn your scent
before any other woman does
i should've carved the truth into your chest
with the blade still lodged in my back
let the blood speak what your mouth never could
and silence pool at your cowardly feet

you made me the grave
i'll make you the ghost
tethered to the ruin you built with my name

// for someone so disposable you sure left quite a mess

i crave your voice
like a drug
i should've died from

but i don't want you back
i want you haunted
i want every new girl to taste me
when she kisses you
and fall into lucid dreams
memories of mine
so she can see what you truly are

i want your mirror to crack
when you say my name
i want your tongue to remember
the taste of my blood

i hope love never feels clean to you again
i want you to lie awake
anguished
wondering how you ruined
the one girl
who would have worshipped you

you lit the match
and i
became the fire

//

you played god with dirty hands
took sick pleasure in my undoing
laughed while i tore myself apart
trying to please you

now i rise
dripping in ash
and every empty apology you choked me with
you don't get to beg
you don't get to look back
i was the fire
you thought you could bury
now i'll smother you in smoke

//

you stare right through my eyes
with the two black holes that occupy your sockets
you cannot comprehend me as a living soul
but i am telling you
begging you
ripping my heart from my chest and holding it up for you to see
please god, just see me
please see who i am
and the shape of who i was supposed to be
acknowledge the damage you have done
the extent of the wounds you've inflicted
that never healed properly
i need you to say it
i need to hear your voice say it
for you to admit that you do not see me as another life
but an energy to deplete
a source to feed the only life that matters
your filthy ego
take my heart from my broken hands
and devour it without a blink

//

you stomp my face into the mud
and i still worship the ground you walk on

//

i've gone mad with whiplash
i would love to hate you
i try so consciously to hate you
but my soul cannot detach
my heart's overthrown my mind

//

we used to hammock by the river
skate for hours in the dark
there was so much desire in your eyes
before your eyes turned to black
and your tongue split in two
before you started lying through your yellow teeth

was what we had not good enough?
what more could you have wanted
than sneaking redds to the rooftop
undressing in the forest
trading deepest darkest secrets through mango clouds
and finding out our souls are entirely the same

how could you forget me so fast

//

growing up
i was taught that nobody likes a taker
so i became a giver
i gave you everything
a safe space
pure devotion
your firstborn child
i gave you my soul

growing up
you were taught selfish survival
you became a taker
you took my heart
my confidence
my family
you took my life

//

forgive me
your highness
for using my tongue to speak
throw me to the gallows
grant me eternal peace

//

this is it
the kingpin
the final boss
armed with a god complex
and nicotine

//

i carved a life out of your chaos
you walked away like it bored you
she won't fix you
she'll just bleed slower
when you finally miss me
don't.
i'm not yours anymore
not even in memory
you created something
that knows how to destroy you
without lifting a finger
i won't come back for you
i'll come for everything you love

//

i wish you the worst
i wish you spider eggs hatching deep within your lungs
the tiny fuzz scattering through your airway
i wish you rats clawing out from underneath your eyelids
those pretty eyelids getting ripped to shreds
i wish you roaches slithering underneath your skin
the crows pecking at your neck to get a taste
death would be too good to you
i wish for you to survive that fate
i wish to see the look in your eyes as you finally
and eternally
feel what you have done to me

// conscious decomposition

all hail our new king
the alpha male
jesus christ himself
sent here to torment me
to make me pay for his sins
all hail the king

// delusions of grandeur

i watched you hold a gun to your head
swing the barrel carelessly through the air
i wasn't thinking about your life
or mine
i wasn't thinking of the unborn baby
all i could think of was her teeth on your neck
that you decided so permanently to destroy your family
that your betrayal did more damage than a bullet ever could

what are you waiting for
pull the trigger

// and a happy due date to you too

may you get all the shameful mediocre sex
your weak heart desires
and every disease that comes with it

//

this is what love becomes
when you poison the roots
and wonder why it stopped growing
releasing toxins
like you were bored
of happily ever after

you blame me for the damage
as you handed me grenades
with the pin already gone
i swallowed them in silence
out of desperation that maybe
my skin could hold your consequences
like it was holding your child
"maybe if i take it on myself"
again
we wouldn't die

i could have been yours
in the kindest way
but you wanted blood
and now you have it
mine
yours
that innocent little boy

you crown yourself father
with your son's bones snapping beneath your feet

//

i will haunt you till the end of your days

//

does it make me a murderer
to wish you had pulled the trigger

//

ghost

the hurricane subsided when they buckled your new anklet
the black band
that keeps your words and fists
far from my skin
the silence was painful at first
like serrated knives tugging at my bones
it became unbearable
i was clawing at my skin
desperate to escape my own existence

and then the silence

the real
true
silence

the peace they describe as what one feels
just before accepting death
it opened my lungs

for the first time in ten years i took a breath
a breath for me
a breath that wasn't weighted down
by the filth of your heavy handed aura
to have you removed from my life so completely
has been so healing

i don't need you
i never did

//

i had fallen so deeply enchanted with your aura
so suddenly and so completely
you were maroon
so mysterious and dark
like smoke spilling through the hall
until i struggled to breathe
you quickly became my oxygen
my body battled relentlessly rejecting this new drug
as i convinced myself time and time again
that this is safe
that you go down easy
like a flaming shot of gasoline

//

if there is a hell
it's shaped like the dark and lonely delivery room
the nurses trying to comfort me
make me feel normal
as if every kind word
wasn't just a neon sign
flashing that you weren't there
that none of this was normal

coming home to sheets you would no longer touch
having family visit and share the experience
and feel nothing but hatred and resentment
because it shouldn't be them
it should have been you

even my boss flew out to meet the new baby
but you couldn't get out of her hand-me-down bed

//

i kept my ring on for months after you cheated
i didn't change my last name
you were my home
you were my person
i dedicated my soul to you
you threw me away like i was single use plastic
and i worshipped you still

//

you were the kid on the playground
with all the superpowers
you've never cared about anyone else
except for what they think of you

//

the last three months have been what i imagine
the very depths of hell to be
a darkness so suffocating and relentless
that i began tearing at my own flesh
fighting to find any escape from the pit
cursing myself because i chose to come here
i chose this pain

and just before i surrendered to the padded white walls
like a lightswitch
the smoke retreated
like a lightswitch
i was finally freed from your spell
and i had forgotten your name

days went by without a trace of you in my life
i could breathe
i could think
i could feel the power and life dripping back into my veins

and then i woke up curled on the floor
the smoke spilling back into my mind
salt crystals tangled in my eyelashes

what happened

cold again and shaking
begging to run back to you just a little
desperate for just a drop of your voice
all i can see is you

please release me

//

i want you to suffer
like i did
silently
eternally
in love with someone
who keeps disappearing

i want you to see me
in every face
that doesn't stay

i loved you
and that love
deserved a better death
than the one you gave it

//

i gave you chances
like they were oxygen
and you used every breath
to curse me for letting you drown

you knew how to swim
but instead you'd swallow the ocean
let the tides fill your lungs
before you'd ever let truth touch you

//

if you asked me back
i'd be there in a heartbeat
let's give it another shot
another shot
another shot
another shot
till i'm sloppy and judgement impaired once again

//

all those nights you gripped my throat
why didn't you just follow through

// the emptiness hurts more than your cruelty ever did

may you carry
every version of me you failed
like diseases from the easy bodies you collect
eternal reminders
eating your flesh away

you don't deserve forgiveness
you don't even deserve memory

// the price of a coward's hunger

you are nothing to me
(please don't go i need you sooooo bad my existence depends on us being together)

//

i wish i could dive into your mind
heal the unholy
i will never leave your side
when i believe your evil nature
is something that can change
that it's an illness
not a choice
that deep
deep
deep
down
the pure essence of your soul still exists
and it is waiting to be rescued

//

your stubbornness wills you
i know you'll miss me
but i also know you'll never let yourself miss me

instead you'll have a black hole commandeering your heart
slowly growing stronger and stronger
and without letting yourself truly understand
you let rage fill its place
until rage consumes you
and it is all you are

so determined to attach my name to all the bad in the world
but it's not that
i'm what's missing inside you
and you know that
and you hate that

the void is screaming
and you work desperately to drown it with captain
to gas it with nicotine
to change reality by telling the world a different story

you can't replace me with your hate
there is no lie you can tell that will mend the broken
you may destroy my reputation
but you'll never heal yourself
and you know that

i do hope badly that you'll come back
not just to me
but to a world where you can no longer cast spells

where reality is reality and it truly is
"as simple as that"
where accountability means something
and isn't just a word you throw around
where you would
finally
be a faithful and equal partner
where i wouldn't be begging for bare minimum
and frenzying over any drop you deal my way

i know you'll never say it out loud
or even let yourself think it
but i know you miss me
i sure as hell miss you

//

we were supposed to make raspberry shakes this weekend
go to the park as a family and give it a real honest go again

but she was more important

so instead
you're eating three day old pizza at a half star motel
the constant reminder of infidelity wrapped around your ankle

i hope she was worth it

//

i should have known
when i had to buy my own ring
and you kept forgetting yours on the counter

//

it is so funny she believes
every single word you say
but i guess i did too

//

one day you'll crack through all that cheap plastic
only to find there is no prize to claim within her

//

i hope it claws through your mind
every time you see a child
with a man who stayed
i hope the weight of what you chose
sits on your chest every night
until it cracks your ribs
night after sleepless night

so here's to every laugh you'll never hear
every birthday you don't earn
every "dad" he saves for someone else

you lost everything
and no one even had to take it from you
you just
torched it
like it was worthless

and that's what you are now

//

you wanted to be a man so badly
you tried to break everything
but yourself

//

i wish i left you on the freeway
the red lights passing but none seem to stop
even if they did it wouldn't matter
not a penny to your name
you destroyed the home you would have gone home to
that is
if you would have been able to find your way back

you
as a parasite
have been leeching my spirit dry
careful not to spill a drop
and i
as a fool
mistook that abuse for love

i'm not sure how or when i woke up
the sunlight doesn't shine around you
i've grown accustomed to your brutality
the birds stopped singing long ago
i think my soul's just run empty
broken down
like the shitty car you didn't tell me about
until after you signed

i hope it eats you alive that you can't be with him
that you'll never know what color his eyes turned to
i hope every father's day twists the knife ever so deeper
this is the life you wanted

//

you're an embarrassment, honestly
nothing but a pathetic boy who tangled my mind
an ungodly infection i chose to display prominently
with the shameful scars i now carry
because i spoke your name
the name that will never touch my lips again
you're a parasite i'm anguished to have ever known
now buried alongside my broken reputation

//

i wish i could give up on you as easily as you gave up on me
that i could just shut it off like a lightswitch like you did
i guess that's the difference between us
i share value with others
and you have no value to share

//

i was so blinded by your charm
i believed every feigned aspiration
all those pretty words
for how you'd change the world
but all you did was waste away on the couch
while you took every penny from my pocket
i was always terrified to ask why
because i could still hear
the foam through your teeth
from the last time i asked

how much more do you need?

//

i deeply miss our friendship
i'm plagued by the weight of this new grief
i miss our romance
but honestly
all the brightest memories are now clouded by your darkness
overgrown with thorns
drowned in your poison
and i just can't go back

//

i always wanted another color
before i knew indigo's name
i wonder what shade you would have been

//

i thought justice was what i need
i've always had a compulsion for equality
definitely to a fault
but justice has been too dark to me
and although the punishment doesn't nearly fit the crime
my heart has been breaking
more than just the damage you inflicted
this weight is too heavy

you've missed so many milestones
sitting
crawling
laughing
autonomy
my heart melts when i watch him
but quickly the joy turns cold
and shatters my lungs

it breaks my heart that i wished justice upon you

although you robbed me of a normal pregnancy
and a normal family
i have now robbed you of fatherhood

//

you spent our hiatus sticking it in anyone who looked your way
watching cheap women online
from the privacy of your own filth

i spent our time apart building a happy
and healthy
home for your son
watching him learn, grow, love
from the safety your absence created

// we are not the same

you don't get to speak my name
like it didn't rot on your tongue
while i begged you to care
you kept me locked in a drawer
alone and unknown
you kissed me like a secret
and left me like a sin
so keep my name
right where you left it
unspoken
and rotting

//

your name
like copper on my tongue
a taste i can never spit out
without also losing a part of myself

you called it passion
i followed along
i couldn't see violence
because violence doesn't kiss
or giggle with me at 3am on our bedroom floor
though i did see
your knuckles still dripping
from the last thing
you swore you loved

i should have known

men like you
make gods of their reflection
and corpses of their lovers

sometimes people rot
even in gardens
sometimes
what was magical
was also mortal

//

i've never belonged in this world
but i did belong in your arms
i belonged in your laughter
your mind
the stars came together just to bring me to you
you were the only thing in this world to ever understand me
and you left

//

i still can't get that sensation out of my mind
my eyes red and hazy
my throat burning and broken
the echoed pain that came with every breath
every swallow
i forgot what birth feels like
but i still remember the crack
your pretty hand wrapping around my neck
the look in your eyes
you kept staring into my eyes
until the black spots removed you from my sight
i'd throw on scarves and hoodies
so you don't have to remember your handiwork
as i remember with every breath

//

what about this am i fighting so hard for?
the ephemeral manias?
the immediate decline of self esteem?
my thoughts beyond distorted to accommodate your reality?
what?

//

i miss those nights we fought way too late
about something that didn't matter
you had to be faultless
i had to be understood
and neither of us could yield
you'd banish me to the bedroom
while you calmed yourself
shooting zombies from the couch

you'd knock on
our
bedroom door
hours later
my eyes still as wide as before
just a little redder now
you'd come sit beside me
without acknowledging
anything
anything
that happened

you'd ask me to 2am coffee
and drive us through the moonlight
with your hand on my leg
it was always the best coffee i've had

i can't drink coffee anymore

why can't i bury what you did
as easily as you did
at the bottom of a diner mug

// waffle house

you expertly crafted a void only you can fill
haunting me
like the imprint you left
on the lonely side of my mattress
i stare into the abyss every night
as i try to shake consciousness from my soul
and still somehow all i see is you
but it's not you
it's the space you used to fill
the aura you used to wear
i am so painfully
and eternally
aware of your absence

they say time will heal
that i just need to learn to love myself
that love will come again
and if not
it's okay to be alone
that i still have my son
my family
my friends

THE AUDACITY

like i'm not missing a vital part of who i am
like i need to replace *you*
like it's okay
like it's going to be okay
like i don't fiercely need that screaming void filled
and silenced

there is not a thing in this world the shape of that void
even if you returned, you are not the same soul you were

it's not okay
it will never be okay

//

you got me hooked
on white powder in a trident wrapper
the love potion you used
to bind me to your cowardly soul
the magic
i thought you were magic
it was just the chemical imbalance in my brain
an imprint you planted
that i slaved relentlessly to strengthen
i fought against myself with each comedown
because sobriety would always make me choose
between the god you were
and reality

//

love is not safe

//

i often find myself looking down the street
watching
waiting
hoping
i'll see your broken down car park in the driveway again

//

i still talk to your ghost
laugh at phantom inside jokes
i whisper them to the walls
in your voice
and smile like you're still here
because even though the devil retches at your heart
my mind only sees you
as the boy who chased me to the elevator
with my lost glove

i still love him

//

blood

how did you look at me
with your blood beneath my skin
and still imagine
your hands belonged to her?

//

he only recognizes your voice
because it screamed at me for nine months
and shook him to the core
the toxic cortisol levels your voice released in me
followed by the hit of dopamine with each empty apology
it's not because he loves you
you made him a crack baby

//

you were never asked
to conquer kingdoms
i had to beg for you
to just
be
here
not even the bare, animal bones
of fatherhood
even wolves provide for their young
but you?
you flinched at the very responsibility
you confidently put in me nine months ago
and left your bloodline to fend without you

you failed
at the one thing
a man is biologically wired to do

//

they call him a shame baby
a bastard son
a title he'll wear unwillingly throughout his days
haunted by whispers of pity
before he can even introduce himself
because you decided to pursue deranged destruction
you mutilated the pure, sacred love
he should have been born into
all for someone who wouldn't even stand out in a lineup of one
with zero character traits and nothing to offer
but a wet spot for your delusional ego
something you already had
you threw him your cross to bear
and he will permanently bear the weight of your devastation
a forever reminder of your sins
when all he should be
is indigo

//

you chose
not to hold him
even when he reached for you

you chose borrowed bodies
who never loved you
over the boy
who would've loved you
forever

you'll tell everyone
i kept you from him
but the truth?

you ran

because i saw you clearly
and he saw you pure
and you couldn't survive either

//

you call yourself a father
i can't even see you as human

//

you didn't just leave
you let him watch
you let him see
what abandonment looks like up close
with my eyes swollen shut from grief
and yours nowhere near the door

you didn't vanish
you fled

he'll remember that
and when he doesn't -
i will.

//

i get so angry when i hear a newborn cry
i missed his life because of you
i'm
still
missing his life because of you

//

i wish you liked your own son even half as much as you

s a l i v a t e

over synthetic eyelashes
the filler in her lips
her breath as fake as your words

how can you clear your schedule for her
quicker than you can beat your own heart
but your mini
your naive flesh and blood
needs to book a time slot in your
"busy"
life
and a time slot in your life
doesn't mean a time slot in your heart
but he doesn't know that yet
and i don't know if i should ever tell him

for your heart
although an ocean
has room for only one
and that is where your ego resides
it expands
to fit the vessel you created
and spills into anyone you recruit
until it smothers them
and they lose themselves trying to accommodate you still

114

i'm trying to find where my soul fled to
i can't let you prey on him too

//

you could've been a father
not just in name
but in presence
protection
effort

but instead
you watched me carry everything
and punished me when i wasn't fathering him properly
then retreated into your goddamn phone
only to return when i once again didn't meet your expectations

you abandoned me to life
and burden
but for him i couldn't skip a beat

our child will know strength
and power

it sure as hell wasn't you

//

tell me what it's like
to have a son
to glorify yourself in being a father
while your son has no idea who you are

//

i am jealous that you
for the rest of your chosen life
get full nights of unbroken sleep
uninterrupted thoughts
that you can do something as simple
as unload a dishwasher
in a matter of minutes
that you could
at the drop of a pin
spontaneously abandon routine
i love him so much
but i am drowning
while you're sleeping peacefully
forgetting you even are a father

//

how am i supposed to be a mom to him when i hurt so bad

//

our son sleeps
with war in his blood
not because he asked for it
but because you
handed him your violence
like a family heirloom

and now he watches the door
for a man who doesn't come
and wonders
if he did something wrong

i carry alone
what you discarded
wrap him in lullabies
so he doesn't scream
when the silence gets too loud

//

you wouldn't hold your own blood
because he needed love
and that asked too much of you
you weren't man enough to give
yet you'd pour it out for empty women
who weren't even worth their dollar store acrylics

you will age into regret
you will hear his name
in rooms you can't enter
you will know what you gave up
as he thrives without you

you are not missed
you are not mourned
you are the curse
you'll carry
until the end

//

may this love never find another
may it rot here
contained
never to touch an innocent throat
never infect a soul too clean to survive it
may the poison stay buried in me
and his blood stay pure
he deserves a world untouched by your devastation
i will burn
before i let him become you

//

i see flashes of another dimension everywhere
shadows of what should have been
he was not built for a one parent home

in every other universe we're all together
and you never betrayed us

i envy it

//

how am i supposed to prioritize myself
while i'm prioritizing our son
by myself

//

he looks just like you
every glance guts what's left of me
same eyes
nose
mouth
how cruel
to be haunted
by something so innocent
to kiss the forehead
of a ghost walking

//

i wonder
do you see him
when you see yourself?
when you wash your face at night
do your eyes meet his?
do they flinch?
do they ask
why you were too weak to stay?
does your reflection
wear the weight of what you abandoned?
the precious little boy you left behind
like trash to the curb

i hope your reflection mocks you
and we all know how often you visit the mirror
you could have been a man
but chose to be a coward
and now he's just another beautiful thing
you will never deserve

//

until you can decide
that your own son
has more value
than mediocre sex with a menopausal mistress
you're not a father
and the fact it's such a difficult choice
proves you'll never be

//

i'll be the parent
you just be…
whatever it is you call this life
the life you chose
the life of no substance
no value
no happiness
the life that was more important
than your own blood

do not come back
not in a year
not in a decade
not when you suddenly decide
you've lived it up enough to turn prodigal
you do not get to say
you are suddenly ready

you do not get to return
to a life you refused to try

//

i have a child to raise
and you have some knots to tie

//

you were supposed to be born
into so much more
and my heart breaks
for all the things
i can no longer give you

if you ever need
you can say it
the name that aches behind your ribs

you're allowed to be angry
you're allowed to miss a man
who doesn't deserve your heart

i'll never ask you
to protect the man
who wouldn't protect you

i will not call you ungrateful
for needing what he wouldn't give

i carried you
i'll carry this with you too
every ache
every question
every piece he dropped

i will hold them
until you're ready to let go

// how am i supposed to tell him his father signed him away
for an xbox

bone

i always thought
well if that was me
i would leave him

until that was me

//

if you truly understood the impact of your actions
the severity of the pain you inflict
you'd run far away, never to return
you could not survive the shame
or bear the weight of accountability
the weight you leave on my shoulders
as you fade away into the sunset

but even just an apology
a grocery store bouquet
a kiss on the forehead
you'd immediately calm the storm
dry my tears
and soften my heart

i am not hard to love
you just won't even try

//

you were counterfeit sapphire
a pirated symbol of truth and faithfulness
and i
amethyst
serenity and peace
believed your fool's impression
until my finger turned green
and you finally showed your true colors
how we blended together as indigo all those years
i'll never know
but i sure miss that shade on you

//

sorry
that you don't take accountability for your own actions
sorry
that your feelings got hurt when i brought up your choices
sorry
that when you tried to kill me i ran for help
sorry
you deserve so much better than that
so please
pursue that empty downgrade
so she can do to you
a sliver of what you've done to me
then you can apologize to her
for her
breaking you

//

growing up, i watched the world through saturated lenses
over the years my eyes became accustomed to those frames
the saturated sight seeped into my mind
and infected the way i view the world still
i do experience things in a saturated hue
intense color and vivid consciousness
you shattered those lenses long ago
but i kept puzzling back the shards
until you kept breaking them
and ground them to dust
now there is nothing but dry golden fields and harsh light
even the green isn't as green
i've always been of the mind
the grass is green where you water it
but what if the water is poisoned

//

you don't love
you perform
you steal personalities
like outfits
mirror them back
and call it connection

then tantrum
when they leave
after meeting the real you
as if there was a you to begin with

//

i think it's funny
for the rest of your chosen life
you have to bear the fact
you have a ten year marriage on your back
and when the next girl
next girl
next girl
next girl
asks
you'll have to explain
why a decade of your life
was very suddenly meaningless

//

sometimes i wonder
if you had died that night
this would all be easier
but that's not something a sane person would ever think
so i guess something's wrong with me too

//

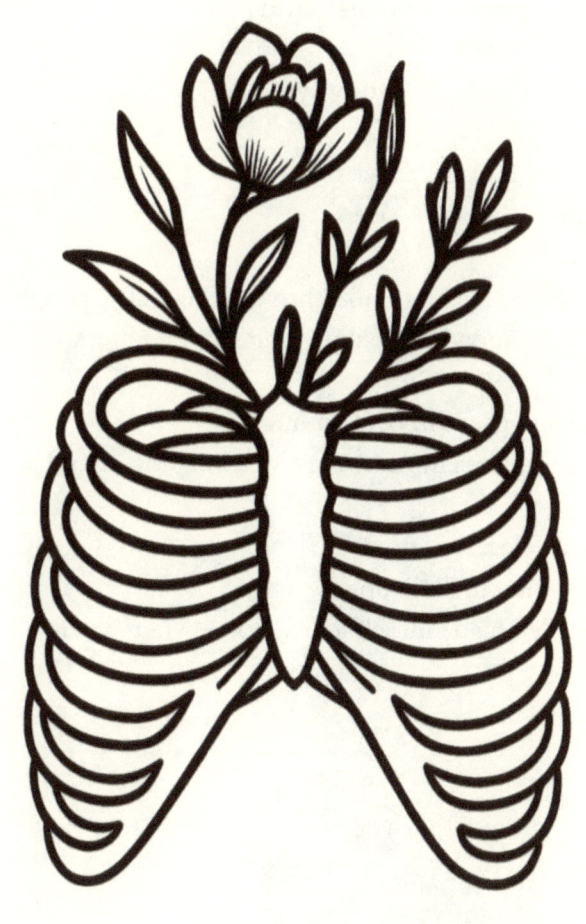

there is a twisted pleasure in darkness
the coldness in my lungs
the numbness in my lips
hitting clouds of electric nicotine
to amplify the ice i feel in my chest
staring at the textures in the ceiling
and pretending i can will myself into not existing
less romanticizing death
and more the idea of nonexistence
to disappear from this world
from myself
in the most selfish of ways

smoke replaces food
caffeine replaces sleep

long and aimless walks through the chilly starlight
i don't know where i'm going and i don't know when i'll be back

finding peace in being numb
inviting the emptiness in like a long lost friend

to be clear
i do long to be happy
but i've made myself a nice home where i'm at

//

i should have left ten years ago
i think i wanted to prove to myself
how unconditionally i could love
how far i could commit beyond reciprocation
love beyond logic
suffer beyond reason
mission accomplished i guess

//

i've been reminiscing
playing everything over and over in my mind
how is it that i've found myself obsessing
romanticizing
the times you assaulted me
the hitting
the spitting
the biting
when you would choke me till i started seeing black spots
till i forgot how to move my body
the feeling of my skull sliding through sheetrock
me showing up to work the next day in long sleeves
in peak summer
protecting your art from others eyes
i left you cute love notes in your lunchbox
you left me a bruised neck, bloodshot eyes, and no voice
you were with me always
and i'd take that again in a heartbeat
because that was the you
before you cheated

// scarves are for hickeys

they say it takes seven attempts
to leave a domestic warzone
but they never mentioned
it's not always the abuser
begging the supply to return
the victim also begs the villain
i begged him so many times
i haven't hit seven yet
is that where stockholm stops?

//

you're as fake as the band that turned my finger green
as empty as the words you've vomited in lieu of any action
as cold as the ice you planted inside my chest
as pathetic as my undying devotion to your vacant potential

//

the ethereal sparkle
glistening through your eyes
was never the love you held for me
it was fireworks from your own soul
to your own soul
glorifying the narcissist you are

it was always you
everything
was always
you

//

you do not love
you love to take

and for ten years i fed you

//

reality cannot be negotiated

//

you were not what i wanted
you were not what i needed
you were an addiction

//

it's been long enough i truly don't believe i'll ever heal
forever cursed to walk through life
with such a vast, decaying wound
my friends keep asking if i'm on the apps yet
like the very thought of a different man on my skin
doesn't make my blood curdle
like my soul doesn't burn at just the idea
of another man getting acquainted with my mind
so incredibly repulsive
i had my life partner
that was you
you destroyed that
i genuinely cannot stomach the idea of loving anyone else
you were it
and you died

//

they keep telling me to "get back out there"
tell me
an animal that's been caged
an animal that's been so abused
so exploited
for so long
what does it do
when it is finally set free

//

you've shown the man you are

someone who could murder his lover
watch me collapse
and not even wipe my blood from the floor

someone who could walk away from his own son
and stay gone
leaving my ghost to raise him

but i still wake up every morning and whisper
"maybe today"
because i loved you deeply
and even though i try to pour more out each day
i still carry as much as i have all these years

you're a man who won't change
and i'm a widow longing for your corpse to return

//

i hate how independent you've trained me to be

//

i don't have the luxury
to waste my life
worshipping a brick wall

//

without your grip on my mind
i'm free to be myself again
to listen again
to understand
to exist in the same reality as everyone else
the reality that yours can't seem to swallow

//

the silence has taught me that my life ultimately is the same
whether you're here or not
if anything
it's been easier
i'm not saying you have nothing to offer
but you sure didn't offer anything to me

//

i don't love you
i'm just lonely
i don't want you in my bed
i just want that void filled
i don't miss the good times
'cause they're strung to the bad
i don't need you
i just need to wake up

//

i want to talk desperately
i crave to peel my skin away
and be terribly
and painfully
vulnerable
i long for 3am conspiracies
and sharing cold pizza on my bedroom floor
for someone to tell me the most monotonous parts of their day
and it be the best part of mine
where friends aren't enough
and family isn't what i need
i am desperate
for connection

//

i am so unbelievably lonely
friends keep reaching out
endlessly bombarded with texts
calls
snapchats
it's exhausting pushing everyone away
how dare you talk to me
can't you see i'm lonely

//

i just want someone to value my existence

//

i honestly have no faith
that i'll find my happily ever after
because even still
after all you've done
all i want
is
you

//

i have seen and lived with the ugliest parts of you
endured the ugliest acts and swallowed your ugliest truths
and i still find you beautiful
a godly being captured within human flesh
if only you could see your divine nature

//

you changed like night and day
but in the sneaking and gradual sense
i'm still so smitten
with the man who swept me off my feet ten years ago
i cannot remotely recognize
the boy who stands before me now

i do not know you anymore
you have immensely devolved
and i hate the monster you've become
the only thing we still have in common
is that you were the only person
either of us ever truly loved
or ever will

i will spend the rest of my days
searching
for where the real you disappeared to

//

it's okay
that i'm lonely
i don't have to force myself
to "find" myself
to "love" myself
to rewire my brain
to pretend that i'm okay

it's okay
to not move on
to let myself be triggered
to envy healthy relationships
healthy families
full, unbroken, families
to grieve what should have been

it's okay
to not want to "enjoy my own company"
day after lonely day
to love my son
but to also dream of escaping this life

i didn't want this
i never would have chosen this
i accept that it happened
but i will not pretend i "enjoy" any of this

it's okay to be bitter
it's okay to be angry
it's okay to not be okay

// stop the toxic propaganda

he really is the sweetest kid
born from the most tumultuous man
he's the calm after your relentless storm
the storm that obliterated his home

he is nothing like you
and you'll never know

//

for my son, and for every child of a mother who had to survive:

cute dude,

i love you so much and i'm so sorry i wasn't able to give you the family you deserve. you are the most perfect thing in this world and you do deserve so much more.

i really did want to be a family, that was always the plan. your dad and i wanted you for a really long time and we were so excited to have a family and all grow old together. i loved your dad so much, and even though he's not here anymore, i still love him more than anything in the world, besides you. i really really wish we could have been a family and it does make me really sad that that didn't get to happen.

your dad and i aren't together anymore because he made some really harmful choices. he hurt me and he tried to hurt you when you were a baby. my job is to keep you safe and loved, and that means sometimes i have to make hard decisions to keep you safe and loved.

there were a lot of things your dad did that weren't okay. hurting people is never something we allow in a family and it's never something we allow in a relationship. i decided we couldn't stay together because you and i both deserve safety, kindness, and love, even if that means our family won't have a dad anymore.

loving someone doesn't mean we accept being hurt by them. i love your dad, but he made a lot of choices that caused a lot of harm. it breaks my heart you'll never meet the good parts of him, but it is safer and happier this way.

you are not the reason your dad left.
you are not the reason your dad isn't here or didn't come back.
you are not the reason for any of this.

your dad left because he just wasn't the kind of grown up that can be in a family, and he couldn't change.

you were always wanted, your dad and me both wanted you so bad.

i will always be honest with you. a lot of this is really hard and sad but i will never lie to you, and i will never get mad at you for any questions you have or feelings you have. it is okay to be angry, at him, at me, at life, you are allowed to feel everything you feel about this. it's really hard and complicated and i want you to know i will always talk about any of this, or we don't have to talk about any of it if you don't want to. i'm here for anything you need and you do not have to go through this alone.

i love you so much

//

//

thank you so much for your support in picking up this book. this collection has been my way of stringing together dark shards of my life into a voice i finally have the strength to use. my goal really is to just make anyone in a similar situation not feel alone. life gets messy and healing is never clean, and my place in my own journey has been anything but perfect, but if you're holding these pages, i hope you find recognition, clarity, or even just a book to pass the time between laundry loads. as much as i am still hurting, i've found pain can be carried and painted into pretty things that help make the burden a little easier.

// aubrey

www.ingramcontent.com/pod-product-compliance
Lightning Source LLC
Chambersburg PA
CBHW031516120626
46545CB00005B/1900